Sleep

Dr. Alvin Silverstein,

Virginia Silverstein, and

Laura Silverstein Nunn

My Health

Franklin Watts

A Division of Grolier Publishing

New York • London • Hong Kong • Sydney

Danbury, Connecticut

Photographs ©: Art Resource, NY: 21 (Tate Gallery, London); Monkmeyer Press: 27 (Paul Gish), 19 (Heron); New England Stock Photo: 4 (Brenda B. James), 40 (Gretchen Palmer), 13 (Frank Siteman); Peter Arnold Inc.: 15 (Laura Dwight), 37 (Helmut Gritscher), 8 top (Robert Holmgren); Photo Researchers: 31 (Tim Davis), 32 (David N. Davis), 7 (F. Hache/Explorer), 22 (Allan Hobson/Science Source), 10, 11 (James Holmes/SPL), 8 bottom (Hank Morgan), 26 (Alfred Pasieka/SPL); PhotoEdit: 35 (J. B. Boykin), 24 (Gary A. Conner), 38 (Mary Kate Denny), 9 (Spencer Grant), 33 (Jonathan Nourok), 14, 16 (David Young-Wolff); Tony Stone Images: 12 left (Lori Adamski), 17 (Geoff Franklin), 29 (Mitch Kezar), 5 (Trevor Mein), 12 right (Ian Shaw).

Visit Franklin Watts on the Internet at:
http://publishing.grolier.com

Library of Congress Cataloging-in-Publication Data

Silverstein, Alvin.
Sleep / by Alvin Silverstein, Virginia Silverstein, and Laura Silverstein Nunn.
        p.   cm.—(My health)
Includes bibliographical references and index.
Summary: Discusses the activities of the body during sleep, the importance of sleep, common sleep disorders, and the phenomenon of dreams.
        ISBN 0-531-11636-0 (lib. bdg.)   0-531-16452-7 (pbk.)
        1. Sleep—Juvenile literature. 2. Sleep disorders—Juvenile literature. [1. Sleep.] I. Silverstein, Virginia B. II. Nunn, Laura Silverstein. III. Title. IV. Series.
QP425.S587   2000
612.8′21—dc21   98-53647
                                                                            CIP
                                                                            AC

Contents

Everybody Sleeps

What would you do if you never had to go to sleep? You could have more time to watch television or play with your toys. And you could spend more time hanging out with your friends. Why should you waste your time sleeping when there's so much for you to do? Actually, you don't have a choice. Your body needs sleep.

Your body is not like the Energizer bunny. It cannot go on and on without stopping. By the end of a day full of action—thinking, moving, eating—you are tired. Sleep may seem like a waste of time, but you need it to re-energize your body. A good night's sleep helps you to grow, regain your strength, and think clearly. Also, it just makes you feel better.

A good night's sleep can help you feel good and stay healthy.
▼

◀ **There are so many fun things to do when you are not sleeping!**

5

Sleep is a natural part of your life, but sometimes you may have trouble sleeping. You can tell when you didn't get a good night's sleep. You still feel tired when you wake up. You may be in a bad mood all day. Your body feels like it is dragging. What can you do to wake up feeling well rested?

Sleep is surely one the world's greatest mysteries. Let's find out more about sleep and why it is so important. What is going on in your body when you sleep? And how can you sleep better?

Did You Know...

People spend about one-third of their lives sleeping. People are not the only living things that sleep. Elephants and eels, birds and butterflies, snakes and salamanders sleep too. Even plants must spend time resting.

What Happens When You Sleep

Have you ever seen somebody else sleeping—your mom or dad or your brother or sister? Sleeping people just lie there. It's almost like they are turned off, the way you would turn off a TV set. Actually, though, there's a lot going on inside them—and you—all the time, even when you're sleeping.

Why Do You Yawn?

Yawning is one of the first signs that you are getting tired. When you start to get sleepy, your breathing rate slows down. Sometimes you may not take in enough oxygen to keep your brain working properly. To get more oxygen, you start to yawn.

Yawning can also be a signal to other people that you are tired or bored. Yawning is catching. Have you ever noticed that you feel like yawning when you see someone else yawn?

Does this picture make you feel sleepy?

Electricity in the Brain

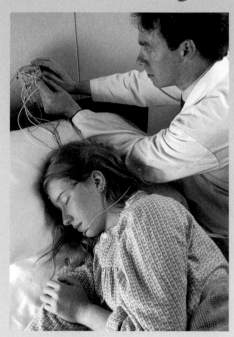

▲
After this girl is hooked up to an EEG machine, a scientist watches her brain waves while she sleeps.
▼

How do scientists know what happens while a person is sleeping? They know that when your brain is working, electric currents flow along your brain cells. (Don't worry—it's only a tiny bit of electricity. It won't hurt you. You can't even feel it.)

Scientists measure the electricity in a person's brain with a machine called an electroencephalograph, or **EEG machine.** The EEG machine traces out a special pattern of wiggly lines that look like waves. Certain kinds of waves can be seen when you are awake and your mind is active. But even when you are sleeping, your mind is still working. Scientists collect information about sleep by studying people while they are sleeping. Can you imagine trying to sleep while you are attached to an EEG machine and someone is watching you?

Nothing seems to be happening while you sleep, but you are going through a series of stages.

You fall asleep in stages, getting deeper and deeper. Stage 1 sleep is the dozing stage—you are not quite awake, but you are not fully asleep either. Your muscles start to relax, and your heart rate and breathing slow down and become very steady. In this stage, you

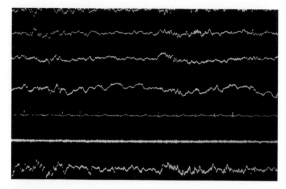

Stage 1

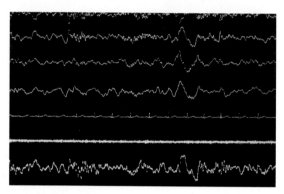

Stage 2

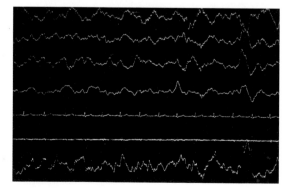

Stage 3

may be partly aware of the world around you.

During Stage 2 sleep, you are really asleep, but it is a very light sleep. Your body becomes more and more relaxed.

As you move into Stages 3 and 4, you fall into a deeper sleep. Your body temperature falls, and your breathing and heart rate slow down. It is hard for someone to wake you up during these stages, and if you do wake up, you'll probably be very groggy.

During the final stage of sleep, your eyes start to move

quickly back and forth while your eyelids are still closed. It is almost as if you were watching a movie—and, in a way, you are. You are dreaming. Scientists call this part of your sleep **REM sleep.** (*REM* comes from the *r*apid *e*ye *m*ovements that occur while you dream.) REM sleep is very different from the other stages of sleep. In REM sleep, your brain becomes more

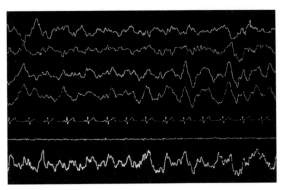

Stage 4

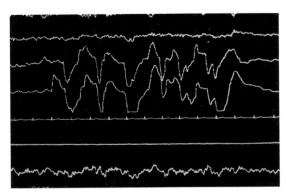

REM sleep

active, your blood pressure rises, and your heartbeat and breathing speed up.

It takes about 90 to 100 minutes to go from Stage 1 to the first period of REM sleep. Scientists call this a **sleep cycle**. You may go through five or six sleep cycles in a night. As the night goes on, your non-REM sleep becomes lighter, and each REM period becomes longer, until you wake up feeling well rested.

Why Do We Need Sleep?

Why is sleep so important? During the day, you spend a lot of time running, jumping, laughing, eating, and talking. You use up a lot of energy, and by the end of the day you're tired. Sleep gives your body a chance

Running and jumping—or just sitting and laughing with a friend—uses up energy.

to rest. But your mind and body are not completely at rest during sleep. They're actually working hard to "recharge your batteries" so that you will wake up feeling good and ready to go.

While you sleep, your brain sorts out all the things that happened during the day. It stores away the important events as memories. It also goes over things you were wondering or worrying about, and you may wake up with answers to some of your problems.

While this girl sleeps, her brain is busy sorting out what happened during the day.

You also grow while you sleep. A chemical called **human growth hormone** is released in the body during sleep to help the growth of cells and tissues. This growth hormone also helps the body to repair itself—to heal cuts, bruises, and sore muscles.

Sleep helps your body to conserve energy too. You use up a lot of energy during your daily activities. But when you sleep, your body temperature falls, and your **metabolism** (the chemical reactions that use up energy in the body) slows down. You are still using some energy, but much less than when you are awake and active.

The hormone that helps you grow is released during sleep.

How Much Sleep Do You Need?

You need different amounts of sleep at different times in your life. A baby may sleep for a total of 16 hours every day. Babies sleep a lot because they are growing so fast. They also have many new experiences to go over—people's faces, voices, colors and shapes, the tastes of foods, or playing with a rattle. Everything is new to a baby.

Children from 6 to 12 years old need an average of 10 to 12 hours of sleep. Teenagers need about 9 to 10 hours of sleep. But many teen-agers don't get enough sleep, so they often feel really tired during the day. Adults need an average of 7 to 8 hours of sleep. Elderly people get the least amount of sleep—not because they need less sleep but because their sleep is often disturbed by aches and pains or having to get up to go to the bathroom.

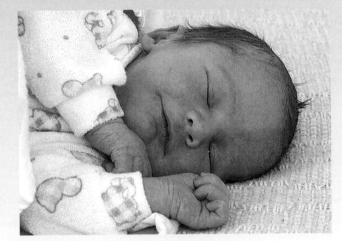

Babies need a lot of sleep.

Have you ever stayed up past your bedtime? Did you get cranky? Did you have trouble getting up the next morning? Maybe you had problems seeing clearly or your mind was in a fog. That was your body's way

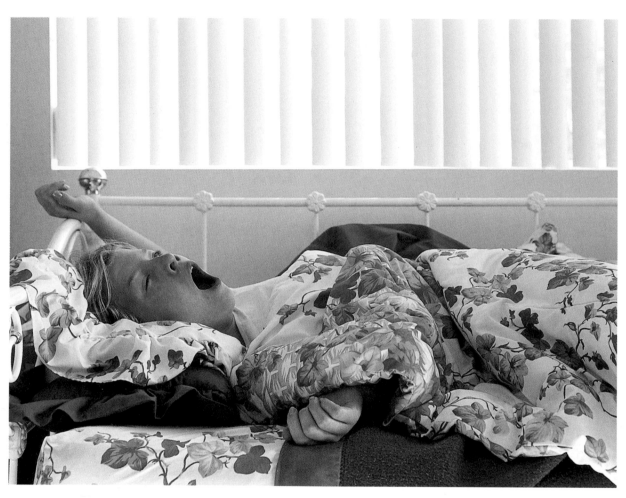

If you haven't had enough sleep, you may feel tired and groggy when you wake up.

of saying, "I need sleep!" Getting the right amount of sleep is very important. A lack of sleep can keep your body and mind from working properly.

The first thing to go is your brain power. A lack of sleep makes it hard to think, concentrate, and remember things. You may find it hard to talk and make deci-

It's hard to think when you haven't been getting enough sleep.

sions. You may be clumsy when you run and jump or write and draw. You may have trouble doing schoolwork. Or you may get very moody. Lack of sleep can make you irritable, depressed, or anxious. Finally, if you don't get enough sleep, you are more likely to get sick. A lack of sleep weakens your body's defenses, which makes it harder to fight off **viruses** and **bacteria.**

Activity 1:
What's Your Sleep Schedule?

Do you have a regular sleep schedule? You can find out by making a record of your sleeping habits. Each day, write down what time you got into bed the night before. Also write down how long it took you to fall asleep and what time you woke up in the morning. Then write down how you felt when you woke up. Were you really tired? Did you have trouble waking up? Or were you well rested and ready to start the day? After a week, look at your sleep schedule. Did you notice that you were more tired when you got less sleep? What can you do to change your sleep schedule so you'll feel better in the morning?

A Look at Dreams

Did you have any dreams last night? Some people say they never dream, but they are mistaken. We all dream every night, but we do not always remember our dreams. You have to wake up at just the right time—during REM sleep—to remember dreams.

Will this girl remember a dream when she wakes up?

19

Dreams are very strange. They seem real, but things happen in dreams that could not happen in real life. You may be able to fly in a dream. Or you  may be at home one minute and halfway around the world the next minute. You have no idea how you got there, and you don't even care.

Did You Know....

People dream during light sleep or deep sleep, but these dreams are very different from the dreams that occur during REM sleep. The light- or deep-sleep dreams are just brief images. REM-sleep dreams are action-packed and filled with emotions.

Many dreams don't make sense. Where do the things you dream about come from? You dream about things that happened to you during the day. You dream about pictures you have seen, stories you have heard, or things you have read. Your brain puts all this information together and makes stories out of it. You can watch these stories in your mind just like you watch a TV show. Some people think there are hidden meanings in our dreams. They say our dreams contain symbols that can help us understand ourselves and the world around us.

What happens when you dream? If someone watched you while you were in REM sleep, you would

This painting by Paul Nash is called "Landscape from a Dream."

be lying perfectly still—except for your eyeballs racing back and forth underneath your eyelids.

Your brain is more active during REM sleep than during any other sleep stage. Your pulse rate, breathing rate, and blood pressure all rise and fall with the action as you dream. Your dreams are often filled with emotion, which causes four times the normal amount of blood to flow to the brain. When you dream, you watch helplessly because your muscles are temporarily paralyzed and you cannot move.

A volunteer in a sleep study drew this picture of a dream.

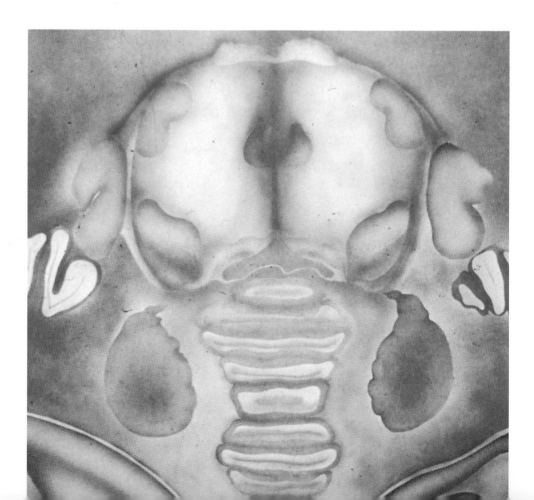

Studies have shown that REM sleep is very important for a good night's sleep. People who were not allowed to enter REM sleep had memory problems. They were also crabby and unable to concentrate after they woke up—even if they slept their usual length of time. People need a good balance of both REM sleep and non-REM sleep.

Activity 2: What Do You Dream?

Do you have trouble remembering your dreams? People often remember a dream when they first wake up, but then get distracted by everyday life. They soon forget the details of their dream. You can remember your dreams by keeping either a tape recorder or a notepad and pencil next to your bed. The moment you wake up, try to remember what you just dreamed and quickly record it or write it down. After a week, look back at what kind of dreams you had. They may tell you a lot about the kind of week you have had, or they might sound like a lot of strange stories.

Do you ever have nightmares? If you do, you're not alone. Everybody has nightmares at some time in their lives. Nightmares are most common in children.

What are nightmares? Nightmares are really bad dreams. They are very scary, powerful, and detailed. Nightmares occur during REM sleep. If you wake up in the middle of one, you can remember it very clearly.

Have you ever seen someone who is sound asleep, but is crying and whining and seems to be having a nightmare? You may be tempted to wake this person up to save him or her from the bad dream. Don't do it. A person who sleeps through a nightmare will not remember it. But if you wake someone

This woman looks like she is having a bad dream.

up during a nightmare, the bad feelings may stay with him or her throughout the day.

People can learn to control their nightmares by changing the story to make it less scary. Some people can even tell themselves to wake up when a dream gets too unpleasant. Fortunately, nightmares are not real, and you will always wake up.

The Clock in Your Body

You may use an alarm clock to wake you up in the morning. But did you know you have a clock inside your body that tells you when to go to sleep and when to get up?

This built-in clock is a special part of your brain, called the **SCN**. Its time is set by messages from your eyes. When sunlight shines in your eyes, your brain knows it is daytime. When it is dark, no light enters your eyes—it is night. The SCN sends messages to a structure deep inside the brain, called the **pineal gland**. It produces a chemical called **melatonin**. When the SCN tells the pineal gland it is dark outside,

This view of the brain shows where the pineal gland is located.

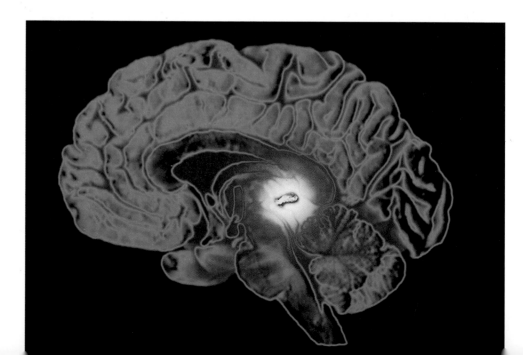

the gland lets melatonin flow into your brain and makes you feel sleepy.

Your built-in **𝐛𝐢𝐨𝐥𝐨𝐠𝐢𝐜𝐚𝐥 𝐜𝐥𝐨𝐜𝐤** is set to the 24-hour cycle of day and night on our planet. Normally, you are wide awake and active during the daytime, and you sleep at night. Your whole body works best during the waking hours. Your muscles are strongest then, your reactions are fastest, and your mind is at its sharpest. Your body temperature also has a 24-hour cycle. It rises

A nap during the afternoon "low" can help restore your energy.

during the daytime when you are active, with a temporary dip in the afternoon. By nighttime, your body temperature begins to drop. It is at its lowest around four o'clock in the morning. After that, the body starts getting ready to wake up.

Not everyone runs on exactly the same biological clock. Most people are ready to get up in the morning, but some people are still feeling low. They don't start to feel energetic until late afternoon or evening. When bedtime comes for most people, these "night owls" are still going strong. If they try to go to bed, they will just lie awake until about two or three o'clock in the morning. That is when their bodies finally feel like going to sleep.

You may think that you are a "morning lark" because you get up early to go to school, but your body may not agree. You may be following a schedule quite different from your body clock. If you didn't have to wake up early for school, or if people could go to work when they wanted to, many people would probably wake up at a later time. But if everyone followed their individual biological clocks, there would be a lot of confusion in the world.

Are You a "Morning Lark" or a "Night Owl?"

Late-night people are often called "night owls" because owls sleep during the day and hunt at night. People who wake up early and feel energetic in the morning are called "morning larks." Larks are birds that wake up early in the morning and sing.

This policeman is hard at work while most people are asleep.

School and most jobs start early in the morning. But some police officers, firefighters, and health-care workers go to work at night when most people are sleeping. And some people must switch frequently from one work shift to another. They work during the daytime on certain days and in the evening or at night

Activity 3: What Does Your Clock Say?

The rising and falling of body temperature is directly related to a person's energy level. As your body temperature rises, so does your energy level. You can find out when you are most active by tracking your body temperature. Take your temperature at certain times of the day. For example, take it when you first wake up, then again at 9:00 a.m., 12:00 p.m., 3:00 p.m., 6:00 p.m., and 9:00 p.m. or when you go to bed. Note what you were doing at these times. Did you feel tired or full of energy? The lower temperatures show when you are least active; the higher ones show when you are most active.

on other days. They may be just getting adjusted to one sleep schedule when they have to change to a different one. This kind of shift work can be very confusing to the

Resetting Your Clock

Do you feel tired and cranky as you begin your week? Many people get the "Monday blues" because their weekday schedule is very different from their weekend schedule. During the week, you have to get up early every morning to go to school. But on the weekend, you are likely to follow your personal biological clock. You probably go to sleep a little later than usual and wake up a little later. Those "Monday blues" are actually your body's response to resetting your biological clock.

You have to get up in time for school, whether your body feels ready or not.

body's inner clock. In fact, many people can never completely adjust to a nighttime work schedule. As a result, workers on the night shift are more likely to make mistakes and have accidents.

Sleep Problems

This girl is having trouble getting to sleep.

For most people, sleep is natural and automatic. Going to sleep is not something they have to think about. They just do it. But for some people, sleeping is not as easy as it looks.

Does it take you a really long time to fall asleep? Do you wake up a lot during the night and have trouble falling back to sleep? Do you wake up easily if you have a stomachache or hear little noises in the room? Do you wake up tired? If so, you're not getting as much sleep as your body needs, and you may have a sleep problem. Everybody has trouble sleeping sometimes, but if these problems go on for several days or weeks and you keep waking up feeling miserable, your sleep problem may be serious.

An **insomniac** is a person who does not get enough deep sleep. In fact, the word *insomnia* means "no sleep." People who have insomnia have trouble falling asleep, staying asleep, or getting a good night's sleep. They sometimes say, "I didn't get a wink of sleep all night." But that's not really true. When people with insomnia are hooked up to an EEG machine, the record of their brain waves usually shows that they are sleeping a normal length of time. But they may sleep lightly and wake up several times during the night. When they get up in the morning, they remember the times they were awake, but not the times they were asleep. So they think they were awake the whole night.

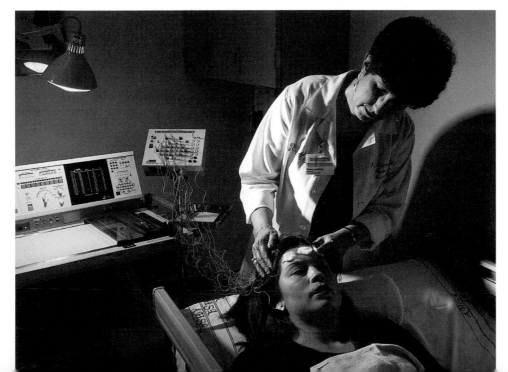

EEG results recorded in a sleep lab usually show that insomniacs sleep a normal length of time.

Breathing is another thing you don't have to think about. Your body just does it. But some people have trouble breathing while they sleep. People with a condition called **sleep apnea** stop breathing during sleep for more than 10 seconds and at least five times each hour. A person who is not breathing is not taking in oxygen, so he or she must wake up to start breathing again. Because sleep is disturbed every time apnea occurs, the person does not wake up feeling rested.

Sleep apnea may be caused by a stopped-up nose or a blocked airpipe in the throat. It may also happen if the brain somehow "forgets" to send the message to breathe. Some people who snore may suffer from sleep apnea. Most children snore now and then, but loud snoring all the time could be a sign of sleep apnea.

Sleepwalking can also be a problem for children. Sleepwalking usually occurs within 1 to 3 hours after falling asleep. It happens during deep, non-REM sleep. Sleepwalkers don't always walk. They may simply sit up in bed and mumble. However, some sleepwalkers open and close drawers or doors, walk up and down stairs,

This boy took his stuffed toy along when he went sleepwalking through the house.

turn on lights, get food and eat it, and go to the bathroom. A few even go outside the house

Sleepwalkers do not usually respond when they are spoken to. Most of them have no memory of sleepwalking when they wake up in the morning. The tendency to sleepwalk may run in families. Children eventually outgrow this condition.

Bedwetting is considered a medical problem if it occurs in children more than 6 years old. Bedwetting is actually a fairly common problem—as many as 7 million children over the age of 6 wet their beds. Bedwetting tends to run in families. If one or both parents wet the bed when they were young, their children are more likely to be bedwetters. Bedwetting may be caused by a variety of things. Some children may not be able to wake themselves out of deep sleep in time to go to the bathroom. Others may have small bladders, so they have to urinate more often. Sometimes stress—at home or at school—can cause a child to wet the bed.

Children who wet the bed often feel embarrassed, guilty, and ashamed. Their fear of bedwetting can turn a restful sleep into a restless sleep. It is important for parents to be understanding. If this problem continues, they should seek help from a doctor.

You wake up suddenly. Your heart is racing, you're sweating, and you're crying. You are feeling really frightened. What's happening? Did you have a nightmare? If you can't remember anything, it may not have been a nightmare. It may have been a **night terror.** Night terrors are sometimes confused with nightmares, but they are very different.

Wetting the bed may make you feel embarrassed and guilty.

Nightmares are vivid bad dreams that occur during REM sleep—usually toward the end of the night. Night terrors occur during deep, non-REM sleep. They usually happen within 1 to 3 hours of going to sleep. When you wake up, you may have no memory of what frightened you. This is because you did not wake up during a dream state. Night terrors are most common in children. Fortunately, children usually grow out of them.

Good Sleeping Habits

What can you do to make sure you get a good night's sleep? You need to develop good sleeping habits.

First, you should have a good sleeping schedule. Try to go to sleep around the same time every night and wake up about the same time every morning.

It's 8 o'clock, and this boy is trying to go to sleep.

(That means keeping to the same schedule on weekends as during the week.) A sleeping schedule that is constantly changing can really wear your body down.

A bedtime routine can also help you get to sleep quickly and easily. What do you do to get ready for bed? You may brush your teeth, get your pajamas on, and read a book in bed or have a story read to you. Having a nightly routine helps your body get ready for what is coming next—sleep!

Good eating habits can also help you sleep well. Don't eat too much candy or drink a lot of cola drinks. These things may make it difficult to settle down. However, a glass of warm milk at bedtime can help you to go to sleep. The warmth is soothing and relaxing, and milk contains a chemical that the body uses to make sleep messages for the brain.

Did You Know...

People who have good sleeping habits are healthier than people with poor sleeping habits. They live longer too.

Exercise can also help you sleep better. You might think that is because it makes you tired, but actually you should not exercise too close to bedtime. Exercise helps to relieve any tension or stress that may keep you awake at night. Studies have shown that exercise helps people fall asleep faster and sleep longer. They also feel better in the morning because they spend more time in deep sleep.

Developing good sleeping habits—and sticking to them—can help you to enjoy a long and healthy life.

Regular exercise helps you to sleep well at night.

Glossary

bacterium (plural **bacteria**)—a microscopic single-celled organism. Some bacteria can cause illness.

bedwetting—unintentional urination while asleep, occurring in someone who is already toilet trained

biological clock—a built-in system that keeps living things in time with the world around them

EEG machine (electroencephalograph)—a device that records electric currents generated by the brain

human growth hormone—a body chemical that stimulates the growth and repair of cells and tissues

insomniac—a person who has difficulty falling asleep or staying asleep for the normal time

melatonin—a chemical produced by the pineal gland. It is released when it is dark and helps make a person sleepy.

metabolism—all the chemical reactions that go on in the body. Most of them use energy, so the *metabolic rate* is a measure of how much energy you are using.

night terror—a sudden, frightening experience that occurs during non-REM sleep and does not involve a vivid dream

pineal gland—a small structure inside the brain that produces a chemical called melatonin. It helps to control processes in the body that go through a regular cycle of changes.

REM sleep—the portions of sleep during which a person dreams; named for the *rapid eye movements* that occur

SCN—the part of the brain that acts as a built-in body clock and helps to control processes that go through a regular cycle of changes; SCN stands for *suprachiasmatic nucleus*

sleep apnea—a condition in which a sleeping person stops breathing for more than 10 seconds, at least five times an hour

sleep cycle—a series of stages, from light into deep sleep, and then into REM sleep (dreaming)

sleepwalking—getting up and walking around or doing other activities without waking up; it occurs during non-REM sleep

virus—a very tiny living thing that feeds on a living host and reproduces by making the host produce new viruses

Learning More

Books

Ancoli-Israel, Sonia. *All I Want Is a Good Night's Sleep*. St. Louis: Mosby, 1996.

Fowler, Allan. *A Good Night's Sleep*. Danbury, CT: Children's Press, 996.

Kastner, Jonathan and Marianna. *Sleep: The Mysterious Third of Your Life*. New York: Harcourt, Brace & World, 1968.

Moore-Ede, Martin, M.D., Ph.D. and Suzanne LeVert. *The Complete Idiot's Guide to Getting a Good Night's Sleep*. New York: Alpha Books (Macmillan), 1998.

Silverstein, Alvin and Virginia. *The Mystery of Sleep*. Boston: Little, Brown, 1987.

Singer, David and William G. Martin. *Sleep on It: A Look at Sleep and Dreams*. Englewood Cliffs, NJ: Prentice-Hall, 1969.

Organizations and Online Sites
The American Sleep Apnea Association (ASAA)
1424 K Street NW, Suite 302
Washington, DC 20005
http://www.sleepapnea.org/

National Foundation for Sleep and Related Disorders in Children
4200 W. Peterson, Suite 109
Chicago, IL 60646

National Sleep Foundation
729 Fifteenth Street, NW, Fourth Floor
Washington, DC 20005
http://www.sleepfoundation.org

SleepNet
http://www.sleepnet.com
This site has the latest information about sleep research.

Sleep Sources
http://bisleep.medsch.ucla.edu/htdocs/hotlinks.html
This site has information about, and Web addresses for, a variety of organizations that study sleep and dreams.

Index

About the Authors

Dr. Alvin Silverstein is a Professor of Biology at the College of Staten Island of the City University of New York. **Virginia Silverstein** is a translator of Russian scientific literature. The Silversteins first worked together on a research project at the University of Pennsylvania. Since then, they have produced six children and more than 150 published books for young people.

Laura Silverstein Nunn, a graduate of Kean College, has been helping with her parents' books since her high school days. She is the coauthor of more than twenty books on diseases and health, science concepts, endangered species, and pets. Laura lives with her husband Matt and their young son Cory in a rural New Jersey town not far from her childhood home.